# 50 Brunch Recipes for the Weekend at Home

By: Kelly Johnson

# Table of Contents

- Eggs Benedict
- Avocado Toast with Poached Eggs
- Blueberry Pancakes
- Breakfast Burritos
- French Toast with Maple Syrup
- Vegetable Frittata
- Cinnamon Rolls
- Huevos Rancheros
- Breakfast Hash with Potatoes and Sausage
- Smoked Salmon Bagels
- Quiche Lorraine
- Belgian Waffles with Berries and Whipped Cream
- Shakshuka
- Banana Bread
- Breakfast Tacos with Chorizo
- Biscuits and Gravy
- Spinach and Mushroom Omelette
- Lemon Ricotta Pancakes
- Breakfast Pizza with Eggs and Bacon
- Greek Yogurt Parfait with Granola and Berries
- Croissant Breakfast Sandwiches
- Sausage and Egg Muffins
- Dutch Baby Pancake
- Breakfast Quesadillas
- Monte Cristo Sandwiches
- Breakfast Cobb Salad
- Cheddar and Chive Biscuits
- Breakfast Stuffed Peppers
- Bagel and Lox Platter
- Lemon Poppy Seed Muffins
- Breakfast Enchiladas
- Asparagus and Goat Cheese Frittata
- Buttermilk Pancakes with Raspberry Compote
- Breakfast Bread Pudding
- Breakfast Sliders with Ham and Cheese

- Apple Cinnamon French Toast Casserole
- Bacon and Egg Breakfast Pizza
- Chia Seed Pudding with Fresh Fruit
- Breakfast Tostadas with Avocado
- Sourdough Pancakes with Honey Butter
- Breakfast Croissant Bake
- Veggie Breakfast Strata
- Pumpkin Spice Waffles
- Breakfast Stuffed Mushrooms
- Breakfast Sausage Rolls
- Coconut Mango Smoothie Bowl
- Cheesy Grits with Shrimp
- Breakfast Empanadas
- Caprese Breakfast Sandwiches
- Nutella Stuffed Pancakes

**Eggs Benedict**

Ingredients:

- 4 large eggs
- 2 English muffins, split and toasted
- 4 slices Canadian bacon or ham
- Hollandaise sauce (see recipe below)
- Chopped parsley, for garnish (optional)

For the Hollandaise Sauce:

- 3 large egg yolks
- 1 tablespoon lemon juice
- 1/2 cup unsalted butter, melted
- Pinch of salt
- Pinch of cayenne pepper (optional)

Instructions:

1. Prepare the hollandaise sauce: In a heatproof bowl, whisk together the egg yolks and lemon juice until thickened and pale in color.
2. Place the bowl over a saucepan of barely simmering water (make sure the bottom of the bowl doesn't touch the water). Whisk constantly until the mixture thickens slightly, about 2 minutes.
3. Slowly drizzle in the melted butter while whisking constantly until the sauce is smooth and thickened. Season with salt and cayenne pepper, if using. Remove from heat and keep warm.
4. In a large skillet, heat some water until simmering. Crack each egg into a small bowl or cup.
5. Carefully slide each egg into the simmering water and poach until the whites are set but the yolks are still runny, about 3-4 minutes. Remove the poached eggs with a slotted spoon and drain on paper towels.
6. While the eggs are poaching, heat the Canadian bacon or ham slices in the skillet until warmed through.

7. To assemble, place a slice of Canadian bacon or ham on each toasted English muffin half. Top with a poached egg, then spoon hollandaise sauce generously over each egg.
8. Garnish with chopped parsley, if desired, and serve immediately.

Enjoy your delicious Eggs Benedict!

**Avocado Toast with Poached Eggs**

Ingredients:

- 2 ripe avocados
- 4 slices of your favorite bread (such as whole grain or sourdough), toasted
- 4 large eggs
- Salt and pepper, to taste
- Optional toppings: sliced cherry tomatoes, red pepper flakes, crumbled feta cheese, chopped fresh herbs (such as cilantro or parsley)

Instructions:

1. Start by poaching the eggs. Fill a medium-sized saucepan with water and bring it to a gentle simmer over medium heat.
2. Crack each egg into a small bowl or cup. This will make it easier to slide them into the water.
3. Once the water is simmering, use a spoon to create a gentle whirlpool in the center of the pot. Carefully slide one egg at a time into the swirling water. Cook for about 3-4 minutes for a runny yolk or longer if you prefer firmer yolks.
4. While the eggs are poaching, prepare the avocado. Cut the avocados in half, remove the pits, and scoop the flesh into a bowl. Mash the avocado with a fork until smooth or leave it slightly chunky, depending on your preference.
5. Season the mashed avocado with salt and pepper to taste. You can also add any optional toppings you like, such as sliced cherry tomatoes or red pepper flakes.
6. Once the eggs are done poaching, use a slotted spoon to carefully remove them from the water and drain any excess water on a clean kitchen towel.
7. Spread the mashed avocado evenly onto the toasted bread slices.
8. Carefully place a poached egg on top of each avocado toast.
9. Season the eggs with a little salt and pepper, and garnish with any additional toppings, if desired.
10. Serve immediately while the eggs are still warm and the toast is crispy.

Enjoy your delicious and nutritious avocado toast with poached eggs!

**Blueberry Pancakes**

Ingredients:

- 1 cup all-purpose flour
- 2 tablespoons granulated sugar
- 1 teaspoon baking powder
- 1/2 teaspoon baking soda
- 1/4 teaspoon salt
- 1 cup buttermilk (or 1 cup milk mixed with 1 tablespoon lemon juice or vinegar, let sit for 5 minutes)
- 1 large egg
- 2 tablespoons unsalted butter, melted
- 1 teaspoon vanilla extract
- 1 cup fresh or frozen blueberries
- Butter or cooking spray, for greasing the pan
- Maple syrup, for serving

Instructions:

1. In a large bowl, whisk together the flour, sugar, baking powder, baking soda, and salt.
2. In another bowl, whisk together the buttermilk, egg, melted butter, and vanilla extract until well combined.
3. Pour the wet ingredients into the dry ingredients and stir until just combined. Be careful not to overmix; it's okay if the batter is slightly lumpy.
4. Gently fold in the blueberries.
5. Heat a non-stick skillet or griddle over medium heat. Add a small amount of butter or spray with cooking spray to lightly grease the surface.
6. Once the skillet is hot, pour about 1/4 cup of batter onto the skillet for each pancake. Use the back of a spoon or a spatula to spread the batter into a round shape if needed.
7. Cook the pancakes for 2-3 minutes, or until bubbles form on the surface and the edges start to look set.
8. Flip the pancakes with a spatula and cook for an additional 1-2 minutes, or until golden brown and cooked through.

9. Transfer the cooked pancakes to a plate and keep warm while you cook the remaining batter, adding more butter or cooking spray to the skillet as needed.
10. Serve the pancakes warm with maple syrup and any other desired toppings, such as additional fresh blueberries or a dusting of powdered sugar.

Enjoy your fluffy and flavorful blueberry pancakes!

**Breakfast Burritos**

Ingredients:

- 4 large eggs
- 1 tablespoon butter or oil
- Salt and pepper, to taste
- 4 large flour tortillas
- 1 cup cooked breakfast meat (such as cooked and crumbled bacon, sausage, or diced ham)
- 1 cup shredded cheese (such as cheddar, Monterey Jack, or Mexican blend)
- 1 cup cooked hash browns or diced potatoes
- Optional fillings: diced bell peppers, onions, jalapeños, diced tomatoes, salsa, avocado slices, sour cream, chopped cilantro

Instructions:

1. In a large skillet, melt the butter or heat the oil over medium heat.
2. In a bowl, beat the eggs with a pinch of salt and pepper.
3. Pour the beaten eggs into the skillet and cook, stirring occasionally, until scrambled and cooked through. Remove from heat and set aside.
4. Warm the flour tortillas in the microwave or on a skillet until soft and pliable.
5. Assemble the burritos: Place a tortilla on a flat surface. Spoon a portion of the scrambled eggs onto the center of the tortilla, followed by a portion of the cooked breakfast meat, shredded cheese, and cooked hash browns or diced potatoes.
6. Add any optional fillings of your choice, such as diced bell peppers, onions, jalapeños, diced tomatoes, salsa, avocado slices, sour cream, or chopped cilantro.
7. Fold the sides of the tortilla over the filling, then roll it up tightly into a burrito shape.
8. Repeat with the remaining tortillas and filling ingredients.
9. If serving immediately, you can warm the assembled burritos in the microwave for 30-60 seconds or in a skillet over medium heat for a few minutes on each side until heated through.

10. Alternatively, you can wrap the burritos individually in foil and store them in the refrigerator or freezer for later use. To reheat, simply unwrap the foil and microwave the burrito until heated through.

Enjoy your homemade breakfast burritos with your favorite toppings and sauces!

**French Toast with Maple Syrup**

Ingredients:

- 4 slices of bread (such as brioche, challah, or French bread), preferably slightly stale
- 2 large eggs
- 1/2 cup milk (whole milk or any milk of your choice)
- 1 teaspoon vanilla extract
- 1/2 teaspoon ground cinnamon
- Butter or cooking spray, for greasing the skillet
- Maple syrup, for serving
- Optional toppings: powdered sugar, fresh berries, sliced bananas, chopped nuts, whipped cream

Instructions:

1. In a shallow dish or pie plate, whisk together the eggs, milk, vanilla extract, and ground cinnamon until well combined.
2. Heat a non-stick skillet or griddle over medium heat. Add a small amount of butter or spray with cooking spray to grease the surface.
3. Dip each slice of bread into the egg mixture, allowing it to soak for a few seconds on each side until well coated but not soggy.
4. Place the soaked bread slices onto the preheated skillet or griddle. Cook for 2-3 minutes on each side, or until golden brown and cooked through.
5. If desired, sprinkle additional cinnamon on top of the cooking French toast for extra flavor.
6. Once cooked, transfer the French toast to serving plates.
7. Serve the French toast warm with maple syrup drizzled over the top.
8. Optionally, garnish with powdered sugar, fresh berries, sliced bananas, chopped nuts, or whipped cream for added sweetness and texture.

Enjoy your delicious French toast with maple syrup for a delightful breakfast or brunch treat!

**Vegetable Frittata**

Ingredients:

- 8 large eggs
- 1/4 cup milk or cream
- Salt and pepper, to taste
- 2 tablespoons olive oil
- 1 small onion, diced
- 1 bell pepper, diced
- 1 cup diced vegetables of your choice (such as spinach, mushrooms, zucchini, tomatoes, broccoli, or asparagus)
- 1/2 cup shredded cheese (such as cheddar, mozzarella, or feta)
- Optional additions: cooked bacon, ham, or sausage
- Fresh herbs, such as parsley or chives, for garnish

Instructions:

1. Preheat your oven to 375°F (190°C).
2. In a large bowl, whisk together the eggs, milk or cream, salt, and pepper until well combined. Set aside.
3. Heat the olive oil in a large oven-safe skillet over medium heat.
4. Add the diced onion and bell pepper to the skillet and cook until softened, about 5 minutes.
5. Add the diced vegetables of your choice to the skillet and cook until they are tender, about 5-7 minutes. If using spinach, add it last and cook just until wilted.
6. If adding cooked bacon, ham, or sausage, add it to the skillet with the vegetables and stir to combine.
7. Once the vegetables are cooked, spread them out evenly in the skillet. Pour the egg mixture over the vegetables.
8. Sprinkle the shredded cheese evenly over the top of the egg mixture.
9. Cook the frittata on the stovetop for 2-3 minutes, or until the edges start to set.
10. Transfer the skillet to the preheated oven and bake for 12-15 minutes, or until the frittata is set in the center and lightly golden on top.
11. Remove the skillet from the oven and let the frittata cool slightly for a few minutes.

12. Carefully slide a spatula around the edges of the frittata to loosen it from the skillet. Slide the frittata onto a cutting board or serving plate.
13. Garnish with fresh herbs, if desired.
14. Slice the frittata into wedges and serve warm or at room temperature.

Enjoy your delicious vegetable frittata as a nutritious and satisfying meal!

**Cinnamon Rolls**

Ingredients:

*For the dough:*

- 1 cup warm milk (around 110°F or 45°C)
- 2 1/4 teaspoons (1 packet) active dry yeast
- 1/2 cup granulated sugar
- 1/3 cup unsalted butter, melted
- 2 large eggs
- 1 teaspoon salt
- 4 to 4 1/2 cups all-purpose flour

*For the filling:*

- 1/2 cup unsalted butter, softened
- 3/4 cup packed brown sugar
- 2 tablespoons ground cinnamon

*For the cream cheese frosting:*

- 4 oz (115g) cream cheese, softened
- 1/4 cup unsalted butter, softened
- 1 teaspoon vanilla extract
- 1 1/2 cups powdered sugar

Instructions:

1. In a mixing bowl, combine warm milk and yeast. Let it sit for about 5 minutes until the yeast is foamy.
2. Add sugar, melted butter, eggs, salt, and 4 cups of flour to the bowl. Mix until the dough starts to come together.

3. Using a dough hook attachment on a stand mixer, knead the dough for about 5-7 minutes until it's smooth and elastic. If the dough is too sticky, gradually add more flour, about 1 tablespoon at a time, until it reaches the right consistency.
4. Transfer the dough to a greased bowl, cover it with a clean kitchen towel or plastic wrap, and let it rise in a warm place for about 1 to 1 1/2 hours, or until it doubles in size.
5. While the dough is rising, prepare the filling by mixing softened butter, brown sugar, and ground cinnamon in a bowl until well combined. Set aside.
6. Once the dough has risen, punch it down and transfer it to a floured surface. Roll out the dough into a large rectangle, about 1/4 inch thick.
7. Spread the cinnamon-sugar filling evenly over the rolled-out dough, leaving a small border around the edges.
8. Starting from one long side, tightly roll up the dough into a log. Pinch the seam to seal.
9. Using a sharp knife or dental floss, cut the dough into 12 equal-sized rolls. Place the rolls into a greased 9x13-inch baking dish, leaving a little space between each roll.
10. Cover the baking dish with a clean kitchen towel or plastic wrap and let the rolls rise in a warm place for another 30-45 minutes, or until they are puffy and doubled in size.
11. Preheat your oven to 350°F (175°C). Once the rolls have risen, bake them in the preheated oven for 20-25 minutes, or until they are golden brown.
12. While the rolls are baking, prepare the cream cheese frosting by mixing softened cream cheese, softened butter, vanilla extract, and powdered sugar in a bowl until smooth and creamy.
13. Remove the cinnamon rolls from the oven and let them cool for a few minutes. Spread the cream cheese frosting over the warm rolls.
14. Serve the cinnamon rolls warm and enjoy!

These homemade cinnamon rolls are sure to be a hit at any brunch or breakfast gathering. Enjoy!

**Huevos Rancheros**

Ingredients:

- 4 large eggs
- 4 corn tortillas
- 1 cup refried beans
- 1 cup salsa (store-bought or homemade)
- 1/2 cup shredded cheese (such as cheddar or Monterey Jack)
- 1 avocado, sliced
- 1/4 cup chopped fresh cilantro
- Lime wedges, for serving
- Salt and pepper, to taste
- Optional toppings: sliced jalapeños, sour cream, diced onions, diced tomatoes

Instructions:

1. Heat a non-stick skillet over medium heat. Warm the tortillas in the skillet for about 1 minute on each side until they are heated through and slightly crispy. Keep the tortillas warm on a plate covered with a clean kitchen towel.
2. In the same skillet, heat the refried beans over medium heat until warmed through. If the beans are too thick, you can thin them out with a little water or broth. Season with salt and pepper to taste.
3. In another skillet, fry the eggs to your desired doneness (such as sunny-side-up or over-easy).
4. To assemble, spread a layer of refried beans onto each warmed tortilla.
5. Top each tortilla with a fried egg.
6. Spoon salsa over the eggs and beans.
7. Sprinkle shredded cheese over the top.
8. Garnish with sliced avocado and chopped cilantro.
9. Serve the huevos rancheros immediately, accompanied by lime wedges for squeezing over the top.
10. Offer additional toppings like sliced jalapeños, sour cream, diced onions, and diced tomatoes for extra flavor and texture.
11. Enjoy your homemade huevos rancheros as a delicious and satisfying breakfast or brunch!

Feel free to customize this recipe according to your taste preferences, adding more or less of each ingredient as desired.

**Breakfast Hash with Potatoes and Sausage**

Ingredients:

- 1 lb (450g) potatoes, diced into small cubes
- 1 lb (450g) breakfast sausage, casings removed
- 1 onion, diced
- 1 bell pepper, diced
- 2 cloves garlic, minced
- 1 teaspoon paprika
- 1/2 teaspoon dried thyme
- Salt and pepper, to taste
- 4 large eggs
- Chopped fresh parsley, for garnish (optional)
- Hot sauce or ketchup, for serving (optional)

Instructions:

1. Heat a large skillet over medium heat. Add the breakfast sausage to the skillet and cook, breaking it up with a spoon, until browned and cooked through. Remove the cooked sausage from the skillet and set aside.
2. In the same skillet, add the diced potatoes. Cook, stirring occasionally, until the potatoes are golden brown and tender, about 10-12 minutes. If the potatoes start to stick to the skillet, you can add a little more oil or butter.
3. Add the diced onion and bell pepper to the skillet with the potatoes. Cook, stirring occasionally, until the vegetables are softened, about 5 minutes.
4. Stir in the minced garlic, paprika, dried thyme, salt, and pepper. Cook for an additional 1-2 minutes, until the garlic is fragrant.
5. Return the cooked sausage to the skillet with the potatoes and vegetables. Stir to combine everything evenly.
6. Using a spoon, make 4 wells in the hash mixture. Crack one egg into each well.
7. Cover the skillet with a lid and cook until the eggs are cooked to your desired doneness, about 5-7 minutes for runny yolks or longer for firmer yolks.
8. Once the eggs are cooked, remove the skillet from the heat. Garnish the breakfast hash with chopped fresh parsley, if desired.
9. Serve the breakfast hash hot, with hot sauce or ketchup on the side if desired.

10. Enjoy your homemade breakfast hash with potatoes and sausage as a delicious and satisfying meal!

Feel free to customize this recipe by adding other ingredients like diced tomatoes, spinach, or cheese, according to your taste preferences.

**Smoked Salmon Bagels**

Ingredients:

- 4 bagels, sliced and toasted
- 8 oz (225g) smoked salmon
- 4 oz (115g) cream cheese, softened
- 1 small red onion, thinly sliced
- Capers, for garnish
- Fresh dill, for garnish
- Lemon wedges, for serving
- Salt and black pepper, to taste

Instructions:

1. Begin by toasting the bagel halves until they are golden brown and crisp. You can toast them in a toaster or under the broiler in the oven.
2. Once the bagels are toasted, spread a generous amount of cream cheese on each bagel half.
3. Arrange slices of smoked salmon on top of the cream cheese-covered bagels.
4. Place a few thinly sliced red onion rings on each bagel half.
5. Sprinkle capers over the smoked salmon and red onions. You can add as many or as few capers as you like, depending on your taste preferences.
6. Garnish each bagel with fresh dill sprigs for added flavor and visual appeal.
7. Season the smoked salmon bagels with a pinch of salt and black pepper, if desired.
8. Serve the smoked salmon bagels immediately, accompanied by lemon wedges for squeezing over the top.
9. Enjoy your homemade smoked salmon bagels as a delicious and elegant breakfast or brunch option!

Feel free to customize this recipe by adding other toppings such as sliced cucumbers, tomatoes, or avocado, according to your taste preferences.

**Quiche Lorraine**

Ingredients:

*For the pie crust:*

- 1 1/4 cups all-purpose flour
- 1/2 teaspoon salt
- 1/2 cup (1 stick) cold unsalted butter, diced
- 1/4 cup ice water

*For the filling:*

- 6 slices bacon, cooked and chopped
- 1 small onion, finely chopped
- 1 cup shredded Gruyère cheese (or Swiss cheese)
- 4 large eggs
- 1 cup heavy cream (or half-and-half)
- 1/2 teaspoon salt
- 1/4 teaspoon black pepper
- 1/4 teaspoon ground nutmeg
- 1 tablespoon chopped fresh parsley (optional)

Instructions:

1. Start by making the pie crust. In a food processor, combine the flour and salt. Add the cold diced butter and pulse until the mixture resembles coarse crumbs.
2. With the food processor running, gradually add the ice water until the dough comes together. Be careful not to overmix. If the dough is too dry, add more ice water, 1 tablespoon at a time.
3. Turn the dough out onto a lightly floured surface and shape it into a disk. Wrap the dough in plastic wrap and refrigerate for at least 30 minutes, or until chilled.
4. Preheat your oven to 375°F (190°C). Roll out the chilled dough on a floured surface into a circle large enough to fit into a 9-inch pie dish. Carefully transfer the dough to the pie dish and gently press it into the bottom and up the sides.

Trim any excess dough and crimp the edges. Prick the bottom of the crust with a fork.

5. Line the pie crust with parchment paper or aluminum foil and fill it with pie weights or dried beans. Blind bake the crust in the preheated oven for 15 minutes. Remove the weights and parchment paper, then continue baking for another 5 minutes, or until the crust is lightly golden. Remove from the oven and set aside.
6. In a skillet, cook the chopped bacon over medium heat until crispy. Remove the bacon from the skillet and drain on paper towels. In the same skillet, sauté the chopped onion until softened and translucent. Remove from heat and set aside.
7. In a bowl, whisk together the eggs, heavy cream, salt, pepper, and nutmeg until well combined.
8. Spread the cooked bacon and sautéed onion evenly over the bottom of the pre-baked pie crust. Sprinkle the shredded Gruyère cheese on top.
9. Pour the egg mixture over the bacon, onion, and cheese in the pie crust.
10. Optional: sprinkle chopped fresh parsley over the top for added flavor and color.
11. Place the quiche in the preheated oven and bake for 35-40 minutes, or until the filling is set and the top is golden brown.
12. Remove the quiche from the oven and let it cool for a few minutes before slicing and serving.
13. Serve the Quiche Lorraine warm or at room temperature, as a delicious breakfast, brunch, or light dinner option.

Enjoy your homemade Quiche Lorraine with its rich and flavorful filling encased in a buttery crust!

**Belgian Waffles with Berries and Whipped Cream**

Ingredients:

*For the waffles:*

- 2 cups all-purpose flour
- 2 tablespoons granulated sugar
- 1 tablespoon baking powder
- 1/2 teaspoon salt
- 2 large eggs, separated
- 1 3/4 cups milk
- 1/2 cup unsalted butter, melted
- 1 teaspoon vanilla extract

*For serving:*

- Fresh berries (such as strawberries, blueberries, raspberries, or blackberries)
- Whipped cream
- Maple syrup or honey, for drizzling
- Powdered sugar, for dusting (optional)

Instructions:

1. Preheat your Belgian waffle maker according to the manufacturer's instructions.
2. In a large bowl, whisk together the flour, sugar, baking powder, and salt.
3. In another bowl, whisk together the egg yolks, milk, melted butter, and vanilla extract until well combined.
4. Pour the wet ingredients into the dry ingredients and stir until just combined. Be careful not to overmix; it's okay if the batter is slightly lumpy.
5. In a clean, dry bowl, beat the egg whites with a hand mixer or stand mixer until stiff peaks form.
6. Gently fold the beaten egg whites into the waffle batter until incorporated. This will help make the waffles light and fluffy.

7. Spray the preheated waffle maker with non-stick cooking spray or brush it with melted butter.
8. Pour enough batter onto the waffle maker to cover the grids, spreading it out evenly. Close the lid and cook the waffles according to the manufacturer's instructions, until they are golden brown and crispy.
9. Once the waffles are cooked, transfer them to a serving plate.
10. Top each waffle with a generous amount of fresh berries and a dollop of whipped cream.
11. Drizzle maple syrup or honey over the waffles, if desired.
12. Optional: dust the waffles with powdered sugar for an extra touch of sweetness.
13. Serve the Belgian waffles with berries and whipped cream immediately, while they are warm and crisp.

Enjoy your homemade Belgian waffles with their golden, crispy exterior and fluffy interior, topped with sweet berries and creamy whipped cream!

**Shakshuka**

Ingredients:

- 2 tablespoons olive oil
- 1 onion, diced
- 1 bell pepper, diced (any color)
- 2 cloves garlic, minced
- 1 teaspoon ground cumin
- 1 teaspoon smoked paprika
- 1/2 teaspoon ground coriander
- 1/4 teaspoon cayenne pepper (optional, for extra heat)
- 1 can (14 oz) diced tomatoes
- 1 can (14 oz) tomato sauce or puree
- Salt and pepper, to taste
- 4-6 large eggs
- Feta cheese, crumbled (optional, for serving)
- Chopped fresh parsley or cilantro, for garnish
- Crusty bread or pita, for serving

Instructions:

1. Heat olive oil in a large skillet or cast iron pan over medium heat.
2. Add diced onion and bell pepper to the skillet. Cook, stirring occasionally, until the vegetables are softened, about 5-7 minutes.
3. Add minced garlic, ground cumin, smoked paprika, ground coriander, and cayenne pepper (if using). Cook, stirring constantly, for about 1 minute until the spices are fragrant.
4. Pour in the diced tomatoes and tomato sauce. Season with salt and pepper to taste. Stir to combine.
5. Simmer the tomato mixture for about 10-15 minutes, stirring occasionally, until it thickens slightly and the flavors meld together.
6. Using a spoon, create small wells in the tomato sauce for the eggs. Crack one egg into each well.
7. Cover the skillet and let the eggs cook in the tomato sauce for about 5-7 minutes, or until the egg whites are set but the yolks are still runny. If you prefer firmer yolks, cook for longer.

8. Once the eggs are cooked to your liking, remove the skillet from heat.
9. Sprinkle crumbled feta cheese over the top, if desired, and garnish with chopped fresh parsley or cilantro.
10. Serve the shakshuka hot, straight from the skillet, with crusty bread or pita on the side for dipping and scooping up the delicious sauce and eggs.

Enjoy your homemade shakshuka as a flavorful and satisfying meal!

**Banana Bread**

Ingredients:

- 2 to 3 ripe bananas, mashed (about 1 cup)
- 1/3 cup melted butter or vegetable oil
- 3/4 cup granulated sugar
- 1 large egg, beaten
- 1 teaspoon vanilla extract
- 1 1/2 cups all-purpose flour
- 1 teaspoon baking soda
- 1/2 teaspoon salt
- Optional mix-ins: chopped nuts (such as walnuts or pecans), chocolate chips, dried fruit (such as raisins or cranberries), or shredded coconut

Instructions:

1. Preheat your oven to 350°F (175°C). Grease a 9x5-inch loaf pan or line it with parchment paper.
2. In a large mixing bowl, mash the ripe bananas with a fork or potato masher until smooth.
3. Stir in the melted butter or oil until well combined with the mashed bananas.
4. Add the granulated sugar, beaten egg, and vanilla extract to the banana mixture. Stir until everything is thoroughly combined.
5. In a separate bowl, whisk together the all-purpose flour, baking soda, and salt.
6. Gradually add the dry ingredients to the wet ingredients, stirring until just combined. Be careful not to overmix; it's okay if there are a few lumps in the batter.
7. If using any optional mix-ins, gently fold them into the batter until evenly distributed.
8. Pour the batter into the prepared loaf pan, spreading it out evenly.
9. Bake the banana bread in the preheated oven for 50 to 60 minutes, or until a toothpick inserted into the center comes out clean.
10. If the top of the banana bread starts to brown too quickly, you can loosely cover it with aluminum foil halfway through baking to prevent over-browning.
11. Once baked, remove the banana bread from the oven and let it cool in the loaf pan for about 10 minutes.

12. After 10 minutes, carefully remove the banana bread from the loaf pan and transfer it to a wire rack to cool completely.
13. Once cooled, slice the banana bread and serve. Enjoy it warm or at room temperature, plain or with a spread of butter or cream cheese.
14. Store any leftover banana bread in an airtight container at room temperature for up to 3 days, or refrigerate it for longer storage.

Enjoy your homemade banana bread, filled with the warm and comforting flavors of ripe bananas!

**Breakfast Tacos with Chorizo**

Ingredients:

- 8 small flour or corn tortillas
- 8 oz (225g) chorizo sausage, casing removed
- 6 large eggs
- Salt and pepper, to taste
- 1 tablespoon butter or oil
- 1 cup shredded cheese (such as cheddar or Monterey Jack)
- Optional toppings: diced avocado, chopped cilantro, salsa, diced tomatoes, sliced jalapeños, sour cream, lime wedges

Instructions:

1. Heat a large skillet over medium heat. Add the chorizo sausage to the skillet, breaking it up with a spoon. Cook the chorizo until it's browned and cooked through, about 5-7 minutes. Remove the cooked chorizo from the skillet and set aside.
2. In a bowl, whisk together the eggs with a pinch of salt and pepper.
3. In the same skillet, melt the butter or heat the oil over medium heat. Pour the beaten eggs into the skillet.
4. Cook the eggs, stirring occasionally, until they are scrambled and just set, about 3-4 minutes. Be careful not to overcook the eggs. Remove from heat.
5. Warm the tortillas in a dry skillet or in the microwave until they are soft and pliable.
6. To assemble the tacos, spoon some of the cooked chorizo onto each tortilla.
7. Top the chorizo with some of the scrambled eggs.
8. Sprinkle shredded cheese over the top of each taco.
9. Add any optional toppings of your choice, such as diced avocado, chopped cilantro, salsa, diced tomatoes, sliced jalapeños, sour cream, or a squeeze of lime juice.
10. Serve the breakfast tacos immediately, while they are warm.

Enjoy your homemade breakfast tacos with chorizo, filled with delicious flavors and customizable toppings!

**Biscuits and Gravy**

Ingredients:

*For the biscuits:*

- 2 cups all-purpose flour
- 1 tablespoon baking powder
- 1/2 teaspoon salt
- 1/2 cup unsalted butter, cold and cut into cubes
- 3/4 cup milk

*For the sausage gravy:*

- 1 lb (450g) breakfast sausage
- 1/4 cup all-purpose flour
- 3 cups milk
- Salt and pepper, to taste

Instructions:

1. Preheat your oven to 425°F (220°C). Line a baking sheet with parchment paper or lightly grease it.
2. In a large mixing bowl, whisk together the flour, baking powder, and salt.
3. Add the cold, cubed butter to the flour mixture. Using a pastry cutter or your fingers, cut the butter into the flour until the mixture resembles coarse crumbs.
4. Gradually pour in the milk, stirring until a soft dough forms. Be careful not to overmix.
5. Turn the dough out onto a lightly floured surface. Pat or roll the dough to about 1/2 inch thick.
6. Use a biscuit cutter or a drinking glass to cut out rounds of dough. Place the biscuits onto the prepared baking sheet.
7. Bake the biscuits in the preheated oven for 12-15 minutes, or until they are golden brown and cooked through.

8. While the biscuits are baking, prepare the sausage gravy. In a large skillet or saucepan, cook the breakfast sausage over medium heat, breaking it up with a spoon, until it is browned and cooked through.
9. Sprinkle the cooked sausage with flour and stir until the flour is fully incorporated and coats the sausage.
10. Gradually pour in the milk, stirring constantly, until the gravy thickens and reaches your desired consistency. Cook the gravy for a few minutes until it is heated through and bubbly.
11. Season the gravy with salt and pepper to taste. Keep warm over low heat until ready to serve.
12. Once the biscuits are done baking, split them open and place them on serving plates.
13. Ladle the warm sausage gravy over the biscuits.
14. Serve the biscuits and gravy hot, as a delicious and satisfying breakfast or brunch dish.

Enjoy your homemade biscuits and gravy, a comforting Southern classic!

**Spinach and Mushroom Omelette**

Ingredients:

- 2 large eggs
- 1 tablespoon milk or water
- Salt and pepper, to taste
- 1/2 tablespoon butter or olive oil
- 1 cup sliced mushrooms
- 1 cup fresh spinach leaves
- 1/4 cup shredded cheese (such as cheddar, Swiss, or feta)
- Optional toppings: diced tomatoes, diced onions, chopped herbs (such as parsley or chives), sliced avocado, salsa

Instructions:

1. In a small bowl, whisk together the eggs, milk or water, salt, and pepper until well combined. Set aside.
2. Heat the butter or olive oil in a non-stick skillet over medium heat.
3. Add the sliced mushrooms to the skillet and cook, stirring occasionally, until they are golden brown and softened, about 5 minutes.
4. Add the fresh spinach leaves to the skillet and cook, stirring occasionally, until they are wilted, about 2-3 minutes. Remove the skillet from heat.
5. Transfer the cooked mushrooms and spinach to a plate and set aside.
6. Return the skillet to the heat and add a little more butter or olive oil if needed.
7. Pour the beaten egg mixture into the skillet, tilting the pan to spread the eggs evenly.
8. As the eggs begin to set around the edges, use a spatula to gently lift the edges and tilt the skillet to allow the uncooked eggs to flow underneath.
9. Once the eggs are mostly set but still slightly runny on top, sprinkle the cooked mushrooms, spinach, and shredded cheese evenly over one half of the omelette.
10. Carefully fold the other half of the omelette over the filling to enclose it.
11. Cook the omelette for another 1-2 minutes, or until the cheese is melted and the eggs are cooked through.
12. Slide the omelette onto a serving plate and garnish with any optional toppings of your choice, such as diced tomatoes, diced onions, chopped herbs, sliced avocado, or salsa.

13. Serve the spinach and mushroom omelette hot, accompanied by toast or your favorite breakfast sides.

Enjoy your homemade spinach and mushroom omelette as a delicious and nutritious breakfast option!

**Lemon Ricotta Pancakes**

Ingredients:

- 1 cup all-purpose flour
- 1 tablespoon granulated sugar
- 1 teaspoon baking powder
- 1/2 teaspoon baking soda
- 1/4 teaspoon salt
- 1 cup ricotta cheese
- 2 large eggs
- 1/2 cup milk
- Zest of 1 lemon
- 2 tablespoons freshly squeezed lemon juice
- 1 teaspoon vanilla extract
- Butter or oil, for cooking
- Maple syrup, fresh berries, and powdered sugar, for serving

Instructions:

1. In a large mixing bowl, whisk together the flour, sugar, baking powder, baking soda, and salt until well combined.
2. In another bowl, combine the ricotta cheese, eggs, milk, lemon zest, lemon juice, and vanilla extract. Mix until smooth and well combined.
3. Pour the wet ingredients into the dry ingredients and stir until just combined. Be careful not to overmix; it's okay if there are a few lumps in the batter.
4. Heat a non-stick skillet or griddle over medium heat. Add a small amount of butter or oil to the skillet to grease it.
5. Pour about 1/4 cup of batter onto the skillet for each pancake. Cook until bubbles form on the surface of the pancake and the edges look set, about 2-3 minutes.
6. Flip the pancakes and cook for an additional 1-2 minutes on the other side, or until golden brown and cooked through.
7. Transfer the cooked pancakes to a plate and keep them warm while you cook the remaining batter. You may need to adjust the heat of the skillet as you go to prevent the pancakes from burning.
8. Serve the lemon ricotta pancakes warm, topped with maple syrup, fresh berries, and a dusting of powdered sugar if desired.

Enjoy your homemade lemon ricotta pancakes as a delicious and indulgent breakfast or brunch treat!

**Breakfast Pizza with Eggs and Bacon**

Ingredients:

*For the pizza dough:*

- 1 pound (about 450g) pizza dough, store-bought or homemade
- Cornmeal or flour, for dusting

*For the toppings:*

- 6 slices bacon, cooked and crumbled
- 4 large eggs
- 1 cup shredded mozzarella cheese
- 1/4 cup grated Parmesan cheese
- 1/2 cup tomato sauce or marinara sauce
- Salt and pepper, to taste
- Chopped fresh parsley or basil, for garnish (optional)

Instructions:

1. Preheat your oven to the highest temperature it can go, usually around 475-500°F (245-260°C). If you have a pizza stone, place it in the oven to preheat as well.
2. Roll out the pizza dough on a lightly floured surface into a circle or rectangle, depending on your preference and the shape of your baking sheet or pizza stone. Dust the surface with cornmeal or flour to prevent sticking.
3. Transfer the rolled-out dough to a baking sheet or pizza peel lined with parchment paper. If using a pizza stone, transfer the dough to the preheated stone.
4. Spread the tomato sauce evenly over the surface of the dough, leaving a small border around the edges.
5. Sprinkle the shredded mozzarella cheese over the tomato sauce.
6. Crack the eggs directly onto the pizza, spacing them evenly apart. You can crack them into small bowls first if you prefer.
7. Sprinkle the crumbled bacon over the pizza, making sure to distribute it evenly.

8. Season the eggs with salt and pepper to taste.
9. Sprinkle the grated Parmesan cheese over the entire pizza.
10. Carefully transfer the pizza to the preheated oven. If using a baking sheet, place it on the middle rack. If using a pizza stone, carefully slide the pizza onto the hot stone in the oven.
11. Bake the pizza for 10-12 minutes, or until the crust is golden brown, the cheese is melted and bubbly, and the eggs are cooked to your desired doneness. Keep an eye on the pizza to prevent burning.
12. Once the pizza is done, remove it from the oven and let it cool slightly.
13. Sprinkle chopped fresh parsley or basil over the top for added flavor and garnish, if desired.
14. Slice the breakfast pizza into wedges and serve hot.

Enjoy your homemade breakfast pizza with eggs and bacon as a delicious and satisfying meal to start your day!

**Greek Yogurt Parfait with Granola and Berries**

Ingredients:

- 1 cup Greek yogurt (plain or flavored, such as vanilla or honey)
- 1/2 cup granola (store-bought or homemade)
- 1/2 cup fresh berries (such as strawberries, blueberries, raspberries, or blackberries)
- 1 tablespoon honey (optional, for drizzling)
- Fresh mint leaves, for garnish (optional)

Instructions:

1. In a serving glass or bowl, layer the ingredients to create the parfait.
2. Start by spooning a layer of Greek yogurt into the bottom of the glass or bowl.
3. Sprinkle a layer of granola over the yogurt.
4. Add a layer of fresh berries on top of the granola.
5. Repeat the layers until you reach the top of the glass or bowl, finishing with a layer of berries.
6. If desired, drizzle a little honey over the top of the parfait for added sweetness.
7. Garnish the parfait with fresh mint leaves for a pop of color and extra flavor, if desired.
8. Serve the Greek yogurt parfait immediately, or refrigerate it for later.
9. Enjoy your homemade Greek yogurt parfait with granola and berries as a delicious and nutritious breakfast, snack, or dessert option!

Feel free to customize this recipe by using different flavors of Greek yogurt, adding other toppings like nuts or seeds, or layering in sliced bananas or other fruits according to your taste preferences.

**Croissant Breakfast Sandwiches**

Ingredients:

- 4 croissants, split in half
- 4 large eggs
- 4 slices of cheese (such as cheddar, Swiss, or Gruyère)
- 8 slices of cooked bacon or ham
- Salt and pepper, to taste
- Butter or oil, for cooking

Optional toppings:

- Sliced tomatoes
- Avocado slices
- Arugula or spinach leaves
- Sliced red onion
- Sriracha or hot sauce
- Mayonnaise or aioli

Instructions:

1. Preheat your oven to 350°F (175°C). Place the split croissants on a baking sheet, cut side up, and toast them in the oven for 5-7 minutes, or until they are lightly golden and crispy. Remove from the oven and set aside.
2. While the croissants are toasting, cook the eggs. Heat a non-stick skillet over medium heat and add a little butter or oil to the pan.
3. Crack the eggs into the skillet and season them with salt and pepper. Cook the eggs to your desired doneness, either frying them sunny-side-up, over-easy, or scrambling them.
4. Once the eggs are cooked, assemble the sandwiches. Place a slice of cheese on the bottom half of each croissant.
5. Top the cheese with a cooked egg, followed by two slices of bacon or ham.
6. Add any optional toppings of your choice, such as sliced tomatoes, avocado slices, arugula or spinach leaves, sliced red onion, sriracha or hot sauce, or mayonnaise or aioli.

7. Place the top half of each croissant on top to form a sandwich.
8. If desired, you can wrap the sandwiches in foil and place them back in the oven for a few minutes to melt the cheese and warm the ingredients.
9. Serve the croissant breakfast sandwiches hot, with your favorite sides such as fresh fruit or a mixed green salad.

Enjoy your homemade croissant breakfast sandwiches as a delicious and satisfying meal to start your day!

**Sausage and Egg Muffins**

Ingredients:

- 6 English muffins, split and toasted
- 6 large eggs
- 6 sausage patties or links, cooked and sliced
- 6 slices of cheese (such as cheddar, American, or Swiss)
- Salt and pepper, to taste
- Butter or oil, for cooking

Optional toppings:

- Sliced tomatoes
- Avocado slices
- Salsa or hot sauce

Instructions:

1. Preheat your oven to 375°F (190°C). Grease a muffin tin with butter or oil, or line it with paper liners.
2. In a large skillet, cook the sausage patties or links according to the package instructions until they are browned and cooked through. Remove from the skillet and set aside.
3. In the same skillet, crack the eggs into the pan and season them with salt and pepper. Cook the eggs to your desired doneness, either frying them sunny-side-up, over-easy, or scrambling them.
4. While the eggs are cooking, place the English muffin halves on a baking sheet. Place a slice of cheese on the bottom half of each English muffin.
5. Once the eggs are cooked, place one cooked egg on top of the cheese on each English muffin.
6. Top each egg with a sliced sausage patty or sausage link.
7. Add any optional toppings of your choice, such as sliced tomatoes, avocado slices, or salsa or hot sauce.
8. Place the top half of each English muffin on top to form a sandwich.

9. If desired, you can wrap each sandwich in foil and store them in the refrigerator for later.
10. To reheat, simply unwrap the sandwiches and microwave them for 1-2 minutes until heated through.
11. Serve the sausage and egg muffins hot, either immediately or as a grab-and-go breakfast option.

Enjoy your homemade sausage and egg muffins as a delicious and satisfying breakfast option that's easy to make ahead of time!

**Dutch Baby Pancake**

Ingredients:

- 3 large eggs
- 1/2 cup all-purpose flour
- 1/2 cup milk
- 2 tablespoons granulated sugar
- 1/2 teaspoon vanilla extract
- 1/4 teaspoon ground cinnamon (optional)
- Pinch of salt
- 2 tablespoons unsalted butter
- Powdered sugar, for dusting (optional)
- Fresh berries, maple syrup, or lemon wedges, for serving

Instructions:

1. Preheat your oven to 425°F (220°C). Place a 10-inch cast iron skillet or oven-safe skillet in the oven while it preheats.
2. In a blender, combine the eggs, flour, milk, granulated sugar, vanilla extract, ground cinnamon (if using), and salt. Blend until smooth and well combined, about 30 seconds.
3. Carefully remove the hot skillet from the oven and add the butter to it. Swirl the skillet to coat the bottom and sides with the melted butter.
4. Pour the batter into the hot skillet over the melted butter. The butter may pool around the edges of the batter, which is okay.
5. Immediately return the skillet to the oven and bake the Dutch baby pancake for 15-20 minutes, or until puffed up and golden brown on the edges. The center may remain slightly soft.
6. Once baked, remove the skillet from the oven. The Dutch baby pancake will deflate slightly as it cools.
7. Dust the Dutch baby pancake with powdered sugar, if desired.
8. Serve the Dutch baby pancake hot, straight from the skillet, with your choice of toppings such as fresh berries, maple syrup, or lemon wedges.
9. Slice the Dutch baby pancake into wedges and enjoy it as a delicious and impressive breakfast or brunch option!

Feel free to customize your Dutch baby pancake by adding other flavorings or toppings such as sliced bananas, chopped nuts, whipped cream, or fruit compote according to your taste preferences.

**Breakfast Quesadillas**

Ingredients:

- 4 large flour tortillas
- 6 large eggs
- 1/4 cup milk
- Salt and pepper, to taste
- 1 tablespoon butter or oil
- 1 cup shredded cheese (such as cheddar, Monterey Jack, or Mexican blend)
- 1 cup cooked breakfast meat (such as cooked and crumbled bacon, sausage, or ham)
- Optional toppings: diced tomatoes, sliced avocado, chopped green onions, salsa, sour cream

Instructions:

1. In a bowl, whisk together the eggs, milk, salt, and pepper until well combined.
2. Heat a large skillet over medium heat and add the butter or oil.
3. Pour the egg mixture into the skillet and cook, stirring occasionally, until the eggs are scrambled and cooked through. Remove from heat and set aside.
4. Wipe out the skillet and return it to the stove over medium heat.
5. Place one flour tortilla in the skillet. Sprinkle half of the tortilla with shredded cheese, cooked breakfast meat, and scrambled eggs.
6. Fold the other half of the tortilla over the filling to create a half-moon shape.
7. Cook the quesadilla for 2-3 minutes on each side, or until golden brown and crispy, and the cheese is melted.
8. Remove the cooked quesadilla from the skillet and repeat the process with the remaining tortillas and filling ingredients.
9. Once all the quesadillas are cooked, slice them into wedges using a sharp knife or pizza cutter.
10. Serve the breakfast quesadillas hot, accompanied by your choice of toppings such as diced tomatoes, sliced avocado, chopped green onions, salsa, or sour cream.

Enjoy your homemade breakfast quesadillas as a delicious and satisfying meal to start your day!

**Monte Cristo Sandwiches**

Ingredients:

- 8 slices of bread (white, wheat, or sourdough)
- 8 slices of cooked ham
- 8 slices of cooked turkey
- 8 slices of Swiss cheese
- Dijon mustard (optional)
- 4 large eggs
- 1/2 cup milk
- Salt and pepper, to taste
- 2 tablespoons butter
- Powdered sugar, for dusting
- Raspberry jam or maple syrup, for dipping

Instructions:

1. Lay out 4 slices of bread on a flat surface. Spread a thin layer of Dijon mustard on each slice, if desired.
2. Top each slice of bread with 2 slices of ham, 2 slices of turkey, and 2 slices of Swiss cheese.
3. Place the remaining 4 slices of bread on top to form sandwiches.
4. In a shallow dish, whisk together the eggs, milk, salt, and pepper until well combined.
5. Heat a large skillet or griddle over medium heat and add 1 tablespoon of butter.
6. Dip each sandwich into the egg mixture, coating both sides evenly.
7. Place the dipped sandwiches in the skillet and cook for 2-3 minutes on each side, or until golden brown and the cheese is melted.
8. Add more butter to the skillet as needed for additional sandwiches.
9. Once cooked, remove the sandwiches from the skillet and let them cool slightly.
10. Slice the Monte Cristo sandwiches diagonally and dust them with powdered sugar.
11. Serve the sandwiches warm, accompanied by raspberry jam or maple syrup for dipping.

Enjoy your homemade Monte Cristo sandwiches as a delicious and indulgent brunch or lunch option!

**Breakfast Cobb Salad**

Ingredients:

- 6 cups mixed salad greens (such as romaine, spinach, or arugula)
- 4 hard-boiled eggs, sliced
- 8 slices cooked bacon, chopped
- 1 cup cherry tomatoes, halved
- 1 avocado, diced
- 1/2 cup crumbled feta or blue cheese
- 1/4 cup sliced green onions
- Salt and pepper, to taste
- Optional toppings: sliced cucumber, bell peppers, shredded carrots

For the dressing:

- 1/4 cup olive oil
- 2 tablespoons red wine vinegar
- 1 teaspoon Dijon mustard
- 1 teaspoon honey or maple syrup
- Salt and pepper, to taste

Instructions:

1. In a large salad bowl, arrange the mixed salad greens as the base of the salad.
2. Arrange the sliced hard-boiled eggs, chopped bacon, cherry tomatoes, diced avocado, crumbled feta or blue cheese, and sliced green onions on top of the greens.
3. Season the salad with salt and pepper to taste.
4. In a small bowl, whisk together the olive oil, red wine vinegar, Dijon mustard, honey or maple syrup, salt, and pepper until well combined to make the dressing.
5. Drizzle the dressing over the salad or serve it on the side.
6. Toss the salad gently to coat all the ingredients with the dressing.
7. Garnish the salad with any optional toppings of your choice, such as sliced cucumber, bell peppers, or shredded carrots.

8. Serve the Breakfast Cobb Salad immediately as a hearty and nutritious breakfast or brunch option.

Enjoy your homemade Breakfast Cobb Salad filled with fresh flavors and wholesome ingredients!

**Cheddar and Chive Biscuits**

Ingredients:

- 2 cups all-purpose flour
- 1 tablespoon baking powder
- 1/2 teaspoon baking soda
- 1/2 teaspoon salt
- 1/2 cup cold unsalted butter, cut into small cubes
- 1 cup shredded cheddar cheese
- 2 tablespoons chopped fresh chives
- 3/4 cup buttermilk (or 3/4 cup milk mixed with 1 tablespoon lemon juice or vinegar, let sit for 5 minutes)

For brushing on top (optional):

- 2 tablespoons melted butter
- 1 tablespoon chopped fresh chives

Instructions:

1. Preheat your oven to 425°F (220°C). Line a baking sheet with parchment paper or lightly grease it.
2. In a large mixing bowl, whisk together the flour, baking powder, baking soda, and salt.
3. Add the cold cubed butter to the flour mixture. Use a pastry cutter or your fingers to work the butter into the flour until the mixture resembles coarse crumbs.
4. Stir in the shredded cheddar cheese and chopped chives until evenly distributed.
5. Make a well in the center of the flour mixture and pour in the buttermilk.
6. Use a spatula or wooden spoon to gently mix the ingredients together until a soft dough forms. Be careful not to overmix.
7. Turn the dough out onto a lightly floured surface. Pat or roll the dough to about 3/4 inch thickness.
8. Use a biscuit cutter or a drinking glass to cut out rounds of dough. Place the biscuits onto the prepared baking sheet, leaving a little space between each one.

9. Gather any scraps of dough, pat them together, and cut out more biscuits until all the dough is used.
10. If desired, brush the tops of the biscuits with melted butter and sprinkle with chopped chives.
11. Bake the biscuits in the preheated oven for 12-15 minutes, or until they are golden brown and cooked through.
12. Remove the biscuits from the oven and let them cool slightly on the baking sheet.
13. Serve the cheddar and chive biscuits warm, as a delicious side dish for breakfast or brunch.

Enjoy your homemade cheddar and chive biscuits, filled with cheesy goodness and savory flavors!

**Breakfast Stuffed Peppers**

Ingredients:

- 4 large bell peppers (any color), halved and seeds removed
- 8 large eggs
- 1 cup cooked breakfast sausage, crumbled
- 1 cup cooked hash browns or diced potatoes
- 1 cup shredded cheddar cheese
- 1/4 cup chopped green onions or chives
- Salt and pepper, to taste
- Cooking spray or olive oil

Instructions:

1. Preheat your oven to 375°F (190°C). Grease a baking dish with cooking spray or olive oil.
2. Place the halved bell peppers in the prepared baking dish, cut side up.
3. In a large mixing bowl, crack the eggs and beat them until well combined. Season with salt and pepper to taste.
4. Stir in the cooked breakfast sausage, cooked hash browns or diced potatoes, shredded cheddar cheese, and chopped green onions or chives into the beaten eggs.
5. Spoon the egg mixture into each bell pepper half, filling them to the top.
6. Cover the baking dish with aluminum foil and bake in the preheated oven for 25-30 minutes, or until the eggs are set and the peppers are tender.
7. Remove the foil and bake for an additional 5-10 minutes, or until the tops are lightly golden and the cheese is melted and bubbly.
8. Once cooked, remove the breakfast stuffed peppers from the oven and let them cool for a few minutes before serving.
9. Serve the breakfast stuffed peppers warm, garnished with additional chopped green onions or chives if desired.

Enjoy your homemade breakfast stuffed peppers as a delicious and satisfying meal to start your day! You can also customize this recipe by adding other ingredients like diced tomatoes, spinach, mushrooms, or cooked bacon according to your taste preferences.

**Bagel and Lox Platter**

Ingredients:

- Bagels (assorted flavors such as plain, sesame, or everything)
- Smoked salmon (lox)
- Cream cheese (plain or flavored)
- Red onion, thinly sliced
- Capers
- Fresh dill, chopped
- Lemon wedges
- Tomatoes, thinly sliced (optional)
- Cucumber, thinly sliced (optional)
- Radishes, thinly sliced (optional)

Instructions:

1. Slice the bagels in half horizontally and toast them lightly, if desired.
2. Spread a generous amount of cream cheese on each half of the bagels.
3. Arrange slices of smoked salmon (lox) on top of the cream cheese.
4. Add thinly sliced red onion rings on top of the salmon.
5. Sprinkle capers and chopped fresh dill over the salmon and onions.
6. Serve lemon wedges on the side for squeezing over the bagels.
7. Arrange additional optional toppings such as thinly sliced tomatoes, cucumbers, and radishes on the platter for variety.
8. Serve the bagel and lox platter immediately, allowing everyone to assemble their own bagels according to their preferences.

Enjoy your homemade bagel and lox platter as a delicious and elegant breakfast or brunch option!

**Lemon Poppy Seed Muffins**

Ingredients:

- 2 cups all-purpose flour
- 1 tablespoon poppy seeds
- 2 teaspoons baking powder
- 1/2 teaspoon baking soda
- 1/4 teaspoon salt
- 1/2 cup unsalted butter, softened
- 1 cup granulated sugar
- 2 large eggs
- 1 teaspoon vanilla extract
- Zest of 2 lemons
- 1/4 cup fresh lemon juice
- 1/2 cup plain Greek yogurt or sour cream

For the glaze (optional):

- 1 cup powdered sugar
- 2-3 tablespoons fresh lemon juice

Instructions:

1. Preheat your oven to 375°F (190°C). Line a muffin tin with paper liners or grease it with butter or non-stick cooking spray.
2. In a medium bowl, whisk together the flour, poppy seeds, baking powder, baking soda, and salt. Set aside.
3. In a large mixing bowl, cream together the softened butter and granulated sugar until light and fluffy.
4. Beat in the eggs one at a time, then add the vanilla extract, lemon zest, and lemon juice. Mix until well combined.
5. Stir in the Greek yogurt or sour cream until smooth.
6. Gradually add the dry ingredients to the wet ingredients, mixing until just combined. Do not overmix.
7. Spoon the batter into the prepared muffin tin, filling each cup about 2/3 full.

8. Bake in the preheated oven for 18-20 minutes, or until a toothpick inserted into the center of a muffin comes out clean.
9. Remove the muffins from the oven and let them cool in the tin for a few minutes before transferring them to a wire rack to cool completely.
10. If desired, prepare the glaze by whisking together the powdered sugar and lemon juice until smooth. Drizzle the glaze over the cooled muffins.
11. Allow the glaze to set before serving the muffins.
12. Enjoy your homemade lemon poppy seed muffins as a delicious breakfast or snack!

These muffins are best enjoyed fresh but can be stored in an airtight container at room temperature for up to 3 days.

**Breakfast Enchiladas**

Ingredients:

- 8 small flour tortillas
- 8 large eggs
- 1/2 cup milk
- Salt and pepper, to taste
- 1 tablespoon butter or oil
- 1 cup cooked breakfast sausage, crumbled
- 1 cup shredded cheddar or Monterey Jack cheese
- 1 cup salsa
- Optional toppings: sliced avocado, chopped cilantro, sour cream, sliced green onions

Instructions:

1. Preheat your oven to 375°F (190°C). Grease a 9x13-inch baking dish with butter or non-stick cooking spray.
2. In a large mixing bowl, whisk together the eggs, milk, salt, and pepper until well combined.
3. Heat the butter or oil in a large skillet over medium heat. Pour the egg mixture into the skillet and cook, stirring occasionally, until the eggs are scrambled and cooked through. Remove from heat and set aside.
4. Lay out the flour tortillas on a flat surface. Divide the scrambled eggs evenly among the tortillas, placing them in a line down the center of each tortilla.
5. Sprinkle the cooked breakfast sausage over the eggs on each tortilla.
6. Sprinkle shredded cheese over the eggs and sausage on each tortilla.
7. Roll up each tortilla tightly and place them seam-side down in the prepared baking dish.
8. Pour the salsa evenly over the top of the rolled enchiladas.
9. Sprinkle any remaining shredded cheese over the top of the enchiladas.
10. Cover the baking dish with aluminum foil and bake in the preheated oven for 20-25 minutes, or until the enchiladas are heated through and the cheese is melted and bubbly.
11. Remove the foil and bake for an additional 5 minutes, or until the cheese is golden brown on top.

12. Remove the breakfast enchiladas from the oven and let them cool slightly before serving.
13. Serve the breakfast enchiladas hot, garnished with sliced avocado, chopped cilantro, sour cream, and sliced green onions, if desired.

Enjoy your homemade breakfast enchiladas as a delicious and hearty meal to start your day!

**Asparagus and Goat Cheese Frittata**

Ingredients:

- 8 large eggs
- 1/4 cup milk or cream
- Salt and pepper, to taste
- 1 tablespoon olive oil
- 1 small onion, diced
- 1 bunch asparagus, tough ends trimmed, and cut into 1-inch pieces
- 4 ounces goat cheese, crumbled
- 2 tablespoons chopped fresh herbs (such as parsley, chives, or dill), optional

Instructions:

1. Preheat your oven to 350°F (175°C).
2. In a large mixing bowl, whisk together the eggs, milk or cream, salt, and pepper until well combined. Set aside.
3. Heat the olive oil in a large oven-safe skillet over medium heat. Add the diced onion and cook until softened, about 3-4 minutes.
4. Add the asparagus pieces to the skillet and cook for an additional 3-4 minutes, or until they are bright green and tender-crisp.
5. Pour the egg mixture evenly over the asparagus and onions in the skillet. Sprinkle the crumbled goat cheese evenly over the top.
6. Cook the frittata on the stovetop for 2-3 minutes, or until the edges begin to set.
7. Transfer the skillet to the preheated oven and bake for 12-15 minutes, or until the frittata is set in the center and lightly golden on top.
8. Remove the skillet from the oven and let the frittata cool for a few minutes.
9. Sprinkle the chopped fresh herbs over the top, if using.
10. Slice the frittata into wedges and serve warm or at room temperature.

Enjoy your homemade asparagus and goat cheese frittata as a delicious and satisfying meal! It pairs well with a side salad or crusty bread.

**Buttermilk Pancakes with Raspberry Compote**

Ingredients:

*For the buttermilk pancakes:*

- 1 cup all-purpose flour
- 2 tablespoons granulated sugar
- 1 teaspoon baking powder
- 1/2 teaspoon baking soda
- 1/4 teaspoon salt
- 1 cup buttermilk
- 1 large egg
- 2 tablespoons unsalted butter, melted
- Butter or oil, for cooking

*For the raspberry compote:*

- 2 cups fresh or frozen raspberries
- 1/4 cup granulated sugar
- 1 tablespoon lemon juice
- 1 teaspoon cornstarch mixed with 1 tablespoon water (optional, for thickening)

Instructions:

1. Prepare the raspberry compote:
    - In a small saucepan, combine the raspberries, sugar, and lemon juice.
    - Cook over medium heat, stirring occasionally, until the raspberries break down and release their juices, and the mixture thickens slightly, about 8-10 minutes.
    - If you prefer a thicker compote, stir in the cornstarch-water mixture and cook for an additional 2-3 minutes, stirring constantly.
    - Remove from heat and let cool slightly.
2. Make the buttermilk pancakes:

- In a large mixing bowl, whisk together the flour, sugar, baking powder, baking soda, and salt.
- In another bowl, whisk together the buttermilk, egg, and melted butter until well combined.
- Pour the wet ingredients into the dry ingredients and stir until just combined. Do not overmix; it's okay if there are a few lumps in the batter.
- Let the batter rest for 5-10 minutes while you preheat your griddle or skillet over medium heat and lightly grease it with butter or oil.
- Pour about 1/4 cup of batter onto the griddle for each pancake. Cook until bubbles form on the surface of the pancakes and the edges look set, about 2-3 minutes.
- Flip the pancakes and cook for an additional 1-2 minutes on the other side, or until golden brown and cooked through.
- Transfer the cooked pancakes to a plate and keep them warm while you cook the remaining batter.

3. Serve:
   - Serve the buttermilk pancakes warm, topped with the raspberry compote.
   - You can also garnish with whipped cream, fresh raspberries, or a dusting of powdered sugar if desired.

Enjoy your homemade buttermilk pancakes with raspberry compote as a delicious and indulgent breakfast treat!

**Breakfast Bread Pudding**

Ingredients:

- 6 cups stale bread cubes (such as French bread or brioche)
- 6 large eggs
- 2 cups milk
- 1/2 cup heavy cream
- 1/2 cup granulated sugar
- 1 teaspoon vanilla extract
- 1/2 teaspoon ground cinnamon
- 1/4 teaspoon ground nutmeg
- Pinch of salt
- 1 cup fresh or frozen berries (such as blueberries, raspberries, or strawberries)
- 1/2 cup chopped nuts (such as pecans or almonds), optional
- Maple syrup or powdered sugar, for serving (optional)

Instructions:

1. Preheat your oven to 350°F (175°C). Grease a 9x13-inch baking dish with butter or non-stick cooking spray.
2. Place the stale bread cubes in the prepared baking dish, spreading them out evenly.
3. In a large mixing bowl, whisk together the eggs, milk, heavy cream, granulated sugar, vanilla extract, ground cinnamon, ground nutmeg, and salt until well combined.
4. Pour the egg mixture over the bread cubes in the baking dish, making sure to coat them evenly. Gently press down on the bread cubes to help them soak up the liquid.
5. Sprinkle the berries and chopped nuts (if using) evenly over the top of the bread mixture.
6. Cover the baking dish with aluminum foil and bake in the preheated oven for 30 minutes.
7. Remove the foil and continue baking for an additional 20-25 minutes, or until the bread pudding is set and golden brown on top.
8. Remove the bread pudding from the oven and let it cool for a few minutes before serving.

9. Serve the breakfast bread pudding warm, drizzled with maple syrup or dusted with powdered sugar if desired.

Enjoy your homemade breakfast bread pudding as a delicious and comforting morning treat! You can also customize it by adding other ingredients like chopped apples, raisins, or chocolate chips according to your taste preferences.

**Breakfast Sliders with Ham and Cheese**

Ingredients:

- 12 slider rolls or dinner rolls, split
- 12 slices of ham
- 6 slices of cheese (such as cheddar, Swiss, or Monterey Jack), halved
- 6 large eggs
- Salt and pepper, to taste
- 2 tablespoons butter
- 1 tablespoon chopped chives or green onions (optional)
- 1 tablespoon sesame seeds (optional)
- 1 tablespoon poppy seeds (optional)
- 1 tablespoon Dijon mustard (optional)
- Maple syrup or honey, for serving (optional)

Instructions:

1. Preheat your oven to 350°F (175°C). Grease a 9x13-inch baking dish or line it with parchment paper.
2. In a skillet, cook the eggs sunny-side-up or scrambled according to your preference. Season with salt and pepper to taste.
3. Place the bottom halves of the slider rolls in the prepared baking dish.
4. Layer each roll with a slice of ham, followed by a slice of cheese, and then a cooked egg.
5. Place the top halves of the slider rolls on top of the eggs to form sandwiches.
6. In a small saucepan, melt the butter over low heat. Stir in the chopped chives or green onions, sesame seeds, poppy seeds, and Dijon mustard if using.
7. Brush the butter mixture evenly over the tops of the slider rolls.
8. Cover the baking dish with aluminum foil and bake in the preheated oven for 15-20 minutes, or until the cheese is melted and the sliders are heated through.
9. Remove the foil and bake for an additional 5 minutes, or until the tops of the sliders are golden brown.
10. Remove the breakfast sliders from the oven and let them cool slightly before serving.
11. Serve the breakfast sliders warm, with maple syrup or honey for dipping if desired.

Enjoy your homemade breakfast sliders with ham and cheese as a delicious and hearty meal to start your day! They're perfect for feeding a crowd or for a family breakfast.

**Apple Cinnamon French Toast Casserole**

Ingredients:

- 1 loaf of French bread, cut into cubes (about 8 cups)
- 4 large eggs
- 1 cup milk
- 1/2 cup heavy cream or half-and-half
- 1/4 cup granulated sugar
- 1 teaspoon vanilla extract
- 1 teaspoon ground cinnamon
- 1/4 teaspoon ground nutmeg
- Pinch of salt
- 2 medium apples, peeled, cored, and thinly sliced
- 2 tablespoons unsalted butter, melted
- 2 tablespoons brown sugar
- Maple syrup, for serving (optional)
- Powdered sugar, for dusting (optional)

Instructions:

1. Preheat your oven to 350°F (175°C). Grease a 9x13-inch baking dish with butter or non-stick cooking spray.
2. Arrange the French bread cubes in the prepared baking dish, spreading them out evenly.
3. In a large mixing bowl, whisk together the eggs, milk, heavy cream or half-and-half, granulated sugar, vanilla extract, ground cinnamon, ground nutmeg, and salt until well combined.
4. Pour the egg mixture over the bread cubes in the baking dish, making sure to coat them evenly. Press down on the bread cubes gently to help them soak up the liquid.
5. In a separate bowl, toss the thinly sliced apples with the melted butter and brown sugar until well coated.
6. Arrange the apple slices evenly over the top of the bread mixture in the baking dish.
7. Cover the baking dish with aluminum foil and bake in the preheated oven for 30 minutes.

8. Remove the foil and bake for an additional 15-20 minutes, or until the French toast casserole is golden brown and set in the center.
9. Remove the casserole from the oven and let it cool for a few minutes before serving.
10. Serve the apple cinnamon French toast casserole warm, drizzled with maple syrup and dusted with powdered sugar if desired.

Enjoy your homemade apple cinnamon French toast casserole as a delicious and indulgent breakfast or brunch dish! It's perfect for serving a crowd or for a cozy family meal.

**Bacon and Egg Breakfast Pizza**

Ingredients:

- 1 pre-made pizza dough (or homemade if you prefer)
- 6 slices of bacon, cooked and crumbled
- 4 large eggs
- 1 cup shredded mozzarella cheese
- 1/4 cup grated Parmesan cheese
- Salt and pepper to taste
- Chopped fresh parsley (optional, for garnish)

Instructions:

1. Preheat your oven according to the pizza dough package instructions or to 425°F (220°C).
2. Roll out the pizza dough onto a baking sheet or pizza stone, forming a circular shape.
3. Sprinkle the shredded mozzarella cheese evenly over the pizza dough, leaving a small border around the edge for the crust.
4. Sprinkle the crumbled bacon over the cheese.
5. Crack the eggs onto the pizza, evenly spacing them apart. You can crack them directly onto the pizza or crack them into a small bowl first and then gently slide them onto the pizza.
6. Sprinkle the grated Parmesan cheese over the eggs and bacon.
7. Season the eggs with salt and pepper to taste.
8. Bake the pizza in the preheated oven for 12-15 minutes, or until the crust is golden brown and the eggs are cooked to your desired level of doneness. Keep an eye on the pizza to prevent overcooking the eggs.
9. Once the pizza is done, remove it from the oven and let it cool slightly.
10. Sprinkle chopped fresh parsley over the top for garnish, if desired.
11. Slice the pizza into wedges and serve hot. Enjoy your delicious bacon and egg breakfast pizza!

**Chia Seed Pudding with Fresh Fruit**

Ingredients:

- 1/4 cup chia seeds
- 1 cup milk (dairy or non-dairy such as almond milk, coconut milk, etc.)
- 1 tablespoon honey or maple syrup (adjust to taste)
- 1/2 teaspoon vanilla extract
- Fresh fruits of your choice (such as berries, sliced bananas, kiwi, mango, etc.)

Instructions:

1. In a mixing bowl or jar, combine the chia seeds, milk, honey or maple syrup, and vanilla extract. Stir well to combine.
2. Let the mixture sit for about 5 minutes, then stir again to break up any clumps of chia seeds.
3. Cover the bowl or jar and refrigerate for at least 2 hours, or preferably overnight, to allow the chia seeds to absorb the liquid and thicken into a pudding-like consistency.
4. Once the chia seed pudding has thickened, give it a good stir to redistribute the seeds.
5. Spoon the pudding into serving bowls or glasses.
6. Top the pudding with fresh fruits of your choice. You can use a single type of fruit or create a colorful mix of different fruits.
7. Serve the chia seed pudding with fresh fruit immediately, or store it covered in the refrigerator for up to 3-4 days.
8. Enjoy your nutritious and delicious chia seed pudding with fresh fruit for breakfast, snack, or dessert!

**Breakfast Tostadas with Avocado**

Ingredients:

- 4 corn tostadas (store-bought or homemade)
- 2 ripe avocados
- 4 eggs
- 1 tablespoon olive oil
- Salt and pepper to taste
- Optional toppings: diced tomatoes, sliced radishes, crumbled queso fresco, chopped cilantro, hot sauce, salsa

Instructions:

1. Begin by preparing the toppings. Peel and pit the avocados, then mash them in a bowl with a fork. Season with salt and pepper to taste. Set aside.
2. Heat olive oil in a skillet over medium heat. Crack the eggs into the skillet and cook them to your desired level of doneness (fried, scrambled, or poached). Season the eggs with salt and pepper while cooking.
3. While the eggs are cooking, warm the corn tostadas in a separate skillet or in the oven according to package instructions until they are heated through and slightly crispy.
4. Once the tostadas are warm, spread a generous layer of mashed avocado onto each one.
5. Place a cooked egg on top of the avocado layer on each tostada.
6. Add any additional toppings you desire, such as diced tomatoes, sliced radishes, crumbled queso fresco, chopped cilantro, hot sauce, or salsa.
7. Serve the breakfast tostadas with avocado immediately while warm.
8. Enjoy your delicious and satisfying breakfast tostadas with avocado! They're perfect for a leisurely weekend brunch or a quick weekday breakfast.

**Sourdough Pancakes with Honey Butter**

Ingredients:

For the pancakes:

- 1 cup sourdough starter
- 1 cup all-purpose flour
- 1 tablespoon sugar
- 1 teaspoon baking soda
- 1/2 teaspoon salt
- 1 egg
- 1 tablespoon melted butter or oil
- 1/2 cup milk (adjust quantity as needed for desired consistency)
- Additional butter or oil for cooking

For the honey butter:

- 1/2 cup (1 stick) unsalted butter, softened
- 2 tablespoons honey

Instructions:

1. In a large mixing bowl, combine the sourdough starter, flour, sugar, baking soda, and salt. Stir until well combined.
2. Add the egg, melted butter or oil, and milk to the bowl. Mix until just combined. The batter should be thick but pourable. If it's too thick, you can add a little more milk until you reach your desired consistency.
3. Heat a non-stick skillet or griddle over medium heat. Add a small amount of butter or oil to the skillet.
4. Pour a portion of the pancake batter onto the skillet, using about 1/4 cup for each pancake. Cook until bubbles form on the surface of the pancake and the edges look set, about 2-3 minutes.
5. Flip the pancake and cook for an additional 1-2 minutes on the other side, or until golden brown and cooked through.

6. Repeat with the remaining batter, adding more butter or oil to the skillet as needed.
7. While the pancakes are cooking, prepare the honey butter. In a small bowl, combine the softened butter and honey. Mix until smooth and well combined.
8. Serve the sourdough pancakes warm, topped with a dollop of honey butter.
9. Enjoy your delicious sourdough pancakes with honey butter for a delightful breakfast or brunch treat!

**Breakfast Croissant Bake**

Ingredients:

- 4 large croissants, sliced in half horizontally
- 6 large eggs
- 1 cup milk
- 1/2 cup shredded cheddar cheese (or cheese of your choice)
- 6 slices cooked bacon, crumbled (or substitute cooked sausage, ham, or vegetarian alternative)
- 1/2 cup diced bell peppers (optional)
- 1/4 cup chopped green onions (optional)
- Salt and pepper to taste
- Butter or cooking spray for greasing the baking dish

Instructions:

1. Preheat your oven to 350°F (175°C). Grease a 9x13 inch baking dish with butter or cooking spray.
2. Arrange the bottom halves of the croissants in the prepared baking dish, cut side up.
3. In a mixing bowl, whisk together the eggs and milk until well combined. Season with salt and pepper to taste.
4. Pour the egg mixture evenly over the croissants in the baking dish.
5. Sprinkle the shredded cheese evenly over the egg mixture.
6. Scatter the crumbled bacon (or other protein), diced bell peppers, and chopped green onions over the cheese.
7. Place the top halves of the croissants over the filling, creating sandwich-like layers.
8. Cover the baking dish with aluminum foil and bake in the preheated oven for 20-25 minutes, or until the eggs are set and the croissants are golden brown.
9. Remove the foil and continue baking for an additional 5-10 minutes to lightly toast the tops of the croissants.
10. Once done, remove the breakfast croissant bake from the oven and let it cool for a few minutes before serving.
11. Slice into portions and serve warm. Enjoy your delicious breakfast croissant bake!

**Veggie Breakfast Strata**

Ingredients:

- 8 slices of bread (such as French bread, sourdough, or whole wheat), cubed
- 1 tablespoon olive oil
- 1 small onion, diced
- 2 cloves garlic, minced
- 2 cups assorted vegetables, chopped (such as bell peppers, spinach, mushrooms, tomatoes, zucchini, etc.)
- 6 large eggs
- 2 cups milk (dairy or non-dairy)
- 1 teaspoon Dijon mustard
- 1/2 teaspoon dried thyme
- 1/2 teaspoon dried oregano
- Salt and pepper to taste
- 1 cup shredded cheese (such as cheddar, Swiss, mozzarella, or a blend)
- Optional toppings: chopped fresh herbs (such as parsley or chives), diced avocado, salsa

Instructions:

1. Preheat your oven to 350°F (175°C). Grease a 9x13 inch baking dish with butter or cooking spray.
2. Heat the olive oil in a skillet over medium heat. Add the diced onion and garlic, and sauté until softened and fragrant, about 2-3 minutes.
3. Add the assorted vegetables to the skillet and cook until tender, about 5-7 minutes. Season with salt and pepper to taste. Remove from heat and let cool slightly.
4. In a large mixing bowl, whisk together the eggs, milk, Dijon mustard, dried thyme, dried oregano, salt, and pepper until well combined.
5. Arrange half of the cubed bread in an even layer in the bottom of the prepared baking dish.
6. Spread the cooked vegetable mixture evenly over the bread.
7. Sprinkle half of the shredded cheese over the vegetables.
8. Arrange the remaining cubed bread on top of the cheese layer.

9. Pour the egg mixture evenly over the bread and vegetables in the baking dish, ensuring that all the bread is soaked in the egg mixture.
10. Sprinkle the remaining shredded cheese over the top of the strata.
11. Cover the baking dish with aluminum foil and bake in the preheated oven for 30 minutes.
12. Remove the foil and continue baking for an additional 15-20 minutes, or until the strata is set and golden brown on top.
13. Once done, remove the veggie breakfast strata from the oven and let it cool for a few minutes before serving.
14. Slice into portions and serve warm, garnished with chopped fresh herbs, diced avocado, or salsa if desired.

Enjoy your delicious and nutritious veggie breakfast strata!

**Pumpkin Spice Waffles**

Ingredients:

- 2 cups all-purpose flour
- 1/4 cup packed brown sugar
- 1 tablespoon baking powder
- 1 teaspoon ground cinnamon
- 1/2 teaspoon ground ginger
- 1/4 teaspoon ground nutmeg
- 1/4 teaspoon ground cloves
- 1/2 teaspoon salt
- 1 and 1/2 cups milk (dairy or non-dairy)
- 1 cup pumpkin puree
- 2 large eggs
- 1/4 cup melted butter or vegetable oil
- 1 teaspoon vanilla extract

Instructions:

1. Preheat your waffle iron according to the manufacturer's instructions.
2. In a large mixing bowl, whisk together the flour, brown sugar, baking powder, cinnamon, ginger, nutmeg, cloves, and salt until well combined.
3. In another bowl, whisk together the milk, pumpkin puree, eggs, melted butter or oil, and vanilla extract until smooth.
4. Pour the wet ingredients into the dry ingredients and mix until just combined. Be careful not to overmix; it's okay if there are a few lumps.
5. Lightly grease the waffle iron with cooking spray or brush with melted butter.
6. Pour the batter onto the preheated waffle iron, using about 1/2 to 3/4 cup of batter per waffle (amount may vary depending on the size of your waffle iron).
7. Close the waffle iron and cook according to the manufacturer's instructions, until the waffles are golden brown and crisp.
8. Carefully remove the waffles from the waffle iron and serve immediately, or keep warm in a low oven until ready to serve.
9. Serve the pumpkin spice waffles with your favorite toppings, such as maple syrup, whipped cream, chopped nuts, or a dusting of powdered sugar.
10. Enjoy your delicious homemade pumpkin spice waffles for a delightful autumn breakfast or brunch!

**Breakfast Stuffed Mushrooms**

Ingredients:

- 8 large mushrooms, cleaned and stems removed
- 4 slices of bacon, cooked and crumbled
- 4 eggs
- 1/4 cup milk
- 1/2 cup shredded cheddar cheese
- 2 green onions, finely chopped
- Salt and pepper to taste
- Fresh parsley, chopped (for garnish)

Instructions:

1. Preheat your oven to 375°F (190°C). Line a baking sheet with parchment paper or lightly grease it with cooking spray.
2. In a bowl, whisk together the eggs and milk until well combined. Season with salt and pepper to taste.
3. Place the mushroom caps on the prepared baking sheet, cavity side up.
4. Divide the crumbled bacon among the mushroom caps, filling each one evenly.
5. Sprinkle shredded cheddar cheese over the bacon in each mushroom cap.
6. Pour the egg mixture evenly into each mushroom cap, filling them to the top.
7. Sprinkle chopped green onions over the top of each stuffed mushroom.
8. Bake in the preheated oven for 15-20 minutes, or until the eggs are set and the mushrooms are tender.
9. Once done, remove the stuffed mushrooms from the oven and let them cool for a few minutes.
10. Garnish with chopped fresh parsley before serving.
11. Serve the breakfast stuffed mushrooms warm as a delicious and satisfying morning meal.

Enjoy your tasty breakfast stuffed mushrooms! They're perfect for a special weekend brunch or a quick and easy weekday breakfast option.

**Breakfast Sausage Rolls**

Ingredients:

- 1 sheet of puff pastry, thawed according to package instructions
- 8 breakfast sausages (pork, chicken, or turkey)
- 1 tablespoon Dijon mustard
- 1 tablespoon maple syrup (optional)
- 1 egg, beaten (for egg wash)
- Sesame seeds or poppy seeds for topping (optional)

Instructions:

1. Preheat your oven to 400°F (200°C). Line a baking sheet with parchment paper or lightly grease it with cooking spray.
2. If your puff pastry is not already rolled out, roll it out on a lightly floured surface into a large rectangle, about 1/4 inch thick.
3. Cut the puff pastry into 8 equal rectangles.
4. In a small bowl, mix together the Dijon mustard and maple syrup (if using).
5. Spread a thin layer of the Dijon mustard mixture onto each puff pastry rectangle.
6. Place a breakfast sausage at one end of each rectangle and roll it up tightly in the puff pastry, sealing the seam.
7. Place the sausage rolls seam-side down on the prepared baking sheet.
8. Brush the tops of the sausage rolls with the beaten egg, then sprinkle with sesame seeds or poppy seeds if desired.
9. Bake in the preheated oven for 20-25 minutes, or until the sausage rolls are golden brown and cooked through.
10. Once done, remove the sausage rolls from the oven and let them cool slightly before serving.
11. Serve the breakfast sausage rolls warm as a delicious and satisfying morning meal or snack.

Enjoy your tasty breakfast sausage rolls! They're perfect for a quick and easy breakfast on the go or a leisurely weekend brunch.

**Coconut Mango Smoothie Bowl**

Ingredients:

For the smoothie base:

- 1 ripe mango, peeled and diced
- 1/2 cup coconut milk (canned or homemade)
- 1/2 cup plain Greek yogurt (or non-dairy yogurt for vegan option)
- 1 tablespoon honey or maple syrup (optional, adjust to taste)
- 1/2 teaspoon vanilla extract (optional)

Toppings:

- Sliced mango
- Toasted coconut flakes
- Fresh berries (such as strawberries, blueberries, or raspberries)
- Chia seeds
- Granola
- Sliced banana
- Mint leaves (for garnish)
- Additional honey or maple syrup for drizzling (optional)

Instructions:

1. In a blender, combine the diced mango, coconut milk, Greek yogurt, honey or maple syrup (if using), and vanilla extract (if using). Blend until smooth and creamy. If the smoothie is too thick, you can add a splash of water or more coconut milk to reach your desired consistency.
2. Pour the smoothie into a bowl.
3. Arrange the sliced mango, toasted coconut flakes, fresh berries, chia seeds, granola, sliced banana, and any other desired toppings on top of the smoothie bowl.
4. Garnish with mint leaves for a fresh touch.
5. Drizzle with additional honey or maple syrup if desired.

6. Serve immediately and enjoy your delicious coconut mango smoothie bowl!

Feel free to customize your smoothie bowl with your favorite fruits, nuts, seeds, and toppings. It's a versatile and nutritious breakfast option that's perfect for starting your day off right.

**Cheesy Grits with Shrimp**

Ingredients:

For the cheesy grits:

- 1 cup stone-ground grits
- 4 cups water
- 1 cup milk
- 1 teaspoon salt
- 1 cup shredded cheddar cheese
- 2 tablespoons unsalted butter
- Salt and pepper to taste

For the shrimp:

- 1 pound large shrimp, peeled and deveined
- 2 tablespoons olive oil
- 2 cloves garlic, minced
- 1/2 teaspoon paprika
- 1/4 teaspoon cayenne pepper (optional, for heat)
- Salt and pepper to taste
- 2 tablespoons fresh lemon juice
- 2 tablespoons chopped fresh parsley

Instructions:

1. To prepare the cheesy grits, bring the water and milk to a boil in a large saucepan over medium-high heat. Stir in the salt.
2. Gradually whisk in the grits, reduce the heat to low, and simmer gently, stirring occasionally, until the grits are thick and creamy, about 20-25 minutes.
3. Stir in the shredded cheddar cheese and butter until melted and well combined. Season with salt and pepper to taste. Keep warm while preparing the shrimp.
4. In a large skillet, heat the olive oil over medium heat. Add the minced garlic and cook until fragrant, about 1 minute.

5. Season the shrimp with paprika, cayenne pepper (if using), salt, and pepper. Add the seasoned shrimp to the skillet in a single layer.
6. Cook the shrimp for 2-3 minutes per side, or until pink and cooked through.
7. Remove the skillet from the heat and squeeze fresh lemon juice over the shrimp. Sprinkle with chopped fresh parsley and toss to coat.
8. To serve, spoon the cheesy grits into bowls and top with the cooked shrimp.
9. Garnish with additional chopped parsley, if desired.
10. Serve immediately and enjoy your delicious cheesy grits with shrimp!

This dish is perfect for a hearty brunch or dinner and is sure to impress with its rich and satisfying flavors.

**Breakfast Empanadas**

Ingredients:

For the dough:

- 2 cups all-purpose flour
- 1/2 teaspoon salt
- 1/2 cup unsalted butter, cold and cubed
- 1/2 cup cold water
- 1 egg (for egg wash)

For the filling:

- 4 eggs
- 1/2 cup cooked breakfast sausage, crumbled
- 1/2 cup shredded cheddar cheese
- Salt and pepper to taste
- Optional additions: diced cooked bacon, diced bell peppers, chopped spinach, diced onions

Instructions:

1. In a large mixing bowl, whisk together the flour and salt.
2. Add the cold, cubed butter to the flour mixture. Using a pastry cutter or your fingertips, work the butter into the flour until the mixture resembles coarse crumbs.
3. Gradually add the cold water, mixing until a dough forms. Be careful not to overmix.
4. Transfer the dough to a lightly floured surface and knead gently until smooth. Wrap the dough in plastic wrap and refrigerate for at least 30 minutes.
5. While the dough is chilling, prepare the filling. In a bowl, whisk the eggs together and season with salt and pepper.

6. In a skillet over medium heat, scramble the eggs until cooked through. Stir in the cooked breakfast sausage and shredded cheddar cheese. Remove from heat and let cool slightly.
7. Preheat your oven to 375°F (190°C). Line a baking sheet with parchment paper.
8. Remove the chilled dough from the refrigerator and roll it out on a lightly floured surface to about 1/4 inch thickness.
9. Use a round cookie cutter or the rim of a glass to cut out circles from the dough.
10. Spoon a small amount of the egg and sausage mixture onto one half of each dough circle, leaving a small border around the edges.
11. Fold the other half of the dough over the filling to create a half-moon shape. Use a fork to crimp the edges and seal the empanadas.
12. Place the assembled empanadas on the prepared baking sheet.
13. Beat the egg for the egg wash and brush it lightly over the tops of the empanadas.
14. Bake in the preheated oven for 20-25 minutes, or until the empanadas are golden brown and crispy.
15. Remove from the oven and let cool for a few minutes before serving.
16. Enjoy your delicious breakfast empanadas warm, either on their own or with your favorite dipping sauce!

These breakfast empanadas are perfect for meal prep or on-the-go mornings, and you can customize the filling to suit your taste preferences.

**Caprese Breakfast Sandwiches**

Ingredients:

- 4 English muffins, split and toasted
- 4 large eggs
- 4 slices fresh mozzarella cheese
- 2 ripe tomatoes, sliced
- Fresh basil leaves
- Balsamic glaze (optional)
- Salt and pepper to taste
- Olive oil or butter for cooking

Instructions:

1. Heat a non-stick skillet over medium heat and add a little olive oil or butter.
2. Crack the eggs into the skillet and cook until the whites are set and the yolks are still runny, or to your desired level of doneness. Season with salt and pepper to taste.
3. While the eggs are cooking, assemble the sandwiches. Place a slice of fresh mozzarella cheese on the bottom half of each English muffin.
4. Top the mozzarella with slices of tomato and fresh basil leaves.
5. Once the eggs are cooked, carefully place one egg on top of each sandwich.
6. Drizzle a little balsamic glaze over the eggs if desired, for an extra burst of flavor.
7. Top each sandwich with the remaining half of the English muffin.
8. Serve the Caprese breakfast sandwiches immediately, while warm.

These sandwiches are a wonderful combination of flavors and textures, with the creamy mozzarella, juicy tomatoes, and fragrant basil. They're perfect for a leisurely weekend brunch or a quick and satisfying breakfast on busy mornings. Enjoy!

**Nutella Stuffed Pancakes**

Ingredients:

- 1 cup all-purpose flour
- 2 tablespoons granulated sugar
- 2 teaspoons baking powder
- 1/2 teaspoon salt
- 1 cup milk
- 1 large egg
- 2 tablespoons unsalted butter, melted
- Nutella or hazelnut chocolate spread
- Optional toppings: sliced bananas, strawberries, whipped cream, powdered sugar

Instructions:

1. In a large mixing bowl, whisk together the flour, sugar, baking powder, and salt until well combined.
2. In a separate bowl, whisk together the milk, egg, and melted butter until smooth.
3. Pour the wet ingredients into the dry ingredients and mix until just combined. Be careful not to overmix; it's okay if there are a few lumps.
4. Heat a non-stick skillet or griddle over medium heat. Lightly grease the skillet with butter or cooking spray.
5. Pour a small amount of pancake batter onto the skillet to form a small pancake, about 3-4 inches in diameter.
6. Spoon a dollop of Nutella onto the center of the pancake.
7. Pour a little more pancake batter over the Nutella to cover it completely.
8. Cook the pancake until bubbles form on the surface and the edges look set, about 2-3 minutes.
9. Carefully flip the pancake and cook for an additional 1-2 minutes on the other side, or until golden brown and cooked through.
10. Repeat with the remaining pancake batter and Nutella, making sure to grease the skillet between batches as needed.
11. Once done, serve the Nutella stuffed pancakes warm.
12. Optionally, top the pancakes with sliced bananas, strawberries, whipped cream, or a dusting of powdered sugar.
13. Enjoy your delicious and indulgent Nutella stuffed pancakes!

These pancakes are sure to be a hit with Nutella lovers of all ages. They're perfect for a special weekend breakfast or brunch treat.